Hoaxing and rumoring in newspaper :a pragmatic study.

Abstract

This research investigates on hoaxing and rumoring by pragmatic analyze, some studies concluded that there are common characteristics in all news which have hoaxing or rumoring. On other side there are hoaxing news could not be detected till their publishers revealed its hoax, such as Alan Sokal hoax which nobody could detect it. This paper is browsing many examples and its pragmatic analyze in order to reach any common characteristics in those articles.

<u>***Introduction***</u>

Newspapers have high popularity in public, which is enabling people to stay abreast of ongoing events and new news. The spread of misinformation is too active in news, where new pieces of information are released piecemeal, often starting off as unverified information in the form of a rumor and hoaxing. These rumors and hoaxing can be spread to large numbers of people, influencing perception and understanding of events, despite being unverified. newspaper is able to prove that those hoaxing and rumors are false, but that are can have harmful consequences both for individuals and for society [3]. For example, A major event that was similarly riddled with consequential rumors was (Tornado Sandy), which hit the East Coast of the US. Part of the city of New York suffered from power outages and many people had to rely on the Internet accessed through their mobile phones for information. To prevent major incidents, the US Federal Emergency Management Agency had to set up a new breaking newspaper specifically for rumor control.

In this research we will define Hoaxing and Rumoring, then

We will try to analyze those terms as discourse analyzing, and we will mention some examples about hoaxing and rumoring in newspaper.

Definition of Hoaxing and Rumoring

A hoax is a trick in which someone tells people a lie, for example that there is a bomb somewhere when there is not, or that a picture is genuine when it is not.

For Example :a series of bomb hoaxes has disrupted Christmas shopping in the city centre.

The word hoax is an industrial-age addition to the English language, according the second edition of the Oxford English dictionary, it first appeared in 1808, just a decade or so before the scientific hoaxes in question began to appear, but the root of the word can be traced back about two hundred years earlier to the phrase (hocus, pocus), apocryphally considered a parody of (hocest corpus) which a Catholic priests would intone during the Eucharist. One of the earliest recorded media hoaxes is a fake almanac published by Jonathan Swift under the pseudonym of Isaac Bickerstaff in 1708.[11] Swift predicted the death of John Partridge, one of the leading astrologers in England at that time, in the almanac and later issued an elegy on the day Partridge was supposed to have died. Partridge's reputation was damaged as a result and his astrological almanac was not published for the next six years.

A **rumor** is a story or piece of information that may or may not be true, but that people are talking about. Or **an unofficial interesting story or piece of news that   might   be true or invented, and quickly spreads from person to person.**

A rumor or rumor is often viewed as "an unverified account or explanation of events circulating from person to person and pertaining to an object, event, or issue in public concern" However, a review of the research on rumor conducted by Pendleton in 1998 , rumor is a concept that lacks a particular definition. But most theories agree that rumor involves some kind of a statement whose veracity is not quickly or ever confirmed. In addition, some scholars have identified rumor as a subset of propaganda, the latter another notoriously difficult concept to define. A pioneer of propaganda studies, (Harold Lasswell) defined propaganda in 1927 as referring "solely to the control of opinion by significant symbols, or, to speak more concretely and less accurately, by stories, rumors, reports, pictures, Rumors are also often discussed with regard to "misinformation" and "disinformation". Rumors thus have often been viewed as particular forms of other communication concepts.

The application of pragmatics in the news

Nowadays scholars mainly make the study of news language from two aspects, to begin with, common linguistics researchers lay their stress on the micro study of pronunciation, words, and words combination. Next, pragmatists beginning with the macro point of view, are liable to analyze elements which could exert their influences to the final linguistic output in news language, and also stress the close connection between language and society. The research of news in terms of pragmatics mainly stay at the study, fuzzy language, the role of direct speech in the news, pragmatic analysis of news language, etc. Up to now, we have not found any related literature about the research on negative news reporting from the perspective of Gricean pragmatic theory.

Now we will try to mention some famous examples about hoaxing in newspaper

In May 1996 physicist Alan Sokal published an essay in the fashionable academic journal Social Text. The essay quoted hip theorists like Jacques Lacan, Donna Haraway, and Gilles Deleuze. The prose was thick with the jargon of poststructuralism. And the point the essay tried to make was counterintuitive: gravity, Sokal argued, was a fiction that society had agreed upon, and science needed to be liberated from its ideological blinders. When Sokal revealed in the pages of Lingua Franca that he had written the article as a parody, the story hit the front page of the New York Times. It set off a national debate still raging today: Are scholars in the humanities trapped in a jargon-ridden Wonderland? Are scientists deluded in thinking their work is objective? Are literature professors suffering from science envy? Was Sokal's joke funny? Was the Enlightenment such a bad thing after all? And isn't it a little bit true that the meaning of gravity is contingent upon your cultural perspective? Collected here for the first time are Sokal's original essay on "quantum gravity," his essay revealing the hoax, the newspaper articles that broke the story, and the angry op-eds, letters, and e-mail exchanges sparked by the hoax from intellectuals across the country, including Stanley Fish, George F. Will, Michael Berube, and Katha Pollitt. Also included are extended essays in which a wide range of scholars ponder the long-term lessons of the hoax.

Content of the article

"Transgressing the Boundaries: Towards a Transformative Hermeneutics of Quantum Gravity" proposed that quantum gravity has progressive political implications, and that the "morphogenetic field" could be a cutting-edge theory of quantum gravity (a morphogenetic field is a concept adapted by Rupert Sheldrake in a way that Sokal characterized in the affair's aftermath as "a bizarre New Age idea"). Sokal wrote that the concept of "an external world whose properties are independent of any individual human being" was "dogma imposed by the long post-Enlightenment hegemony over the Western intellectual outlook".

After referring skeptically to the "so-called scientific method", the article declared that "it is becoming increasingly apparent that physical 'reality'" is fundamentally "a social and linguistic construct". It went on to state that because scientific research is "inherently theory-laden and self-referential", it "cannot assert a privileged epistemological status with respect to counter hegemonic narratives emanating from dissident or marginalized communities" and that therefore a "liberatory science" and an "emancipatory mathematics", spurning "the elite caste canon of 'high science'", needed to be established for a "postmodern science [that] provide[s] powerful intellectual support for the progressive political project".

Publication

Sokal submitted the article to Social Text, whose editors were collecting articles for the "Science Wars" issue. "Transgressing the Boundaries: Towards a Transformative Hermeneutics of Quantum Gravity" was the only article submitted by a natural scientist. Later, after Sokal's self-exposure of his pseudoscientific hoax article in the journal Lingua Franca, the Social Text editors said in a published essay that they had requested editorial changes that Sokal refused to make, and had had concerns about the quality of the writing, stating "We requested him (a) to excise a good deal of the philosophical speculation and (b) to excise most of his footnotes Nonetheless, despite subsequently designating the physicist as having been a "difficult, uncooperative author", and noting that such writers were "well known to journal editors", Social Text published the article in acknowledgment of the author's credentials in the May 1996 Spring/Summer "Science Wars" issue. The editors did not seek peer review of the article by physicists or otherwise; they later defended this decision on the basis that Social Text was a journal for open intellectual inquiry and the article was not offered as a contribution to the physics discipline.

Now we note that Sokal cast himself as a leftist (which he is in real life) by claiming to embark on the project of creating a "liberatory" science that could resist and eventually supplant capitalist science (1996a, p. 226). This stance clearly fits the profile of the typical *Social Text* article.

Furthermore, Sokal forecasts a "truly progressive science" that will serve the "radical democratization of all aspects of social, economic, political, and cultural life" (p. 229). Radical democracy is Stanley Aronowitz's principal political program (Martin, 1995, p. 102). Thus, Sokal made specific efforts in choosing his rhetorical ideology to flatter *Social Text*'s most important advisor. Sokal frames his article as an evaluation of the principles of the new science of quantum gravity according to radical democratic ideals for a progressive science (p. 218). This topos of evaluation is the most frequent high-level organizer in the sample of *Social Text*'s articles.

Sokal paid close attention to the low-level rhetoric, syntax, and lexicon of *Social Text* articles in creating his hoax.

Syntax: Sokal used long, complex sentences with heavy nominalization, highly typical in *Social Text* pieces, as in this example from his opening paragraph as follow:

"Rather, [natural scientists] cling to the dogma imposed by the long post-Enlightenment hegemony over the Western intellectual outlook, which can be summarized briefly as follows: that there exists an external world, whose properties are independent of any individual human being and indeed of humanity as a whole: that these properties are encoded in "eternal" physical laws; and that human beings can obtain reliable, albeit imperfect and tentative, knowledge of these laws by hewing to the "objective" procedures and epistemological strictures prescribed by the (so-called) scientific method. (p. 217)

• Qualification: As evinced by the above excerpt, Sokal frequently employed hedges and qualifications typical of cultural studies rhetoric. "(So-called) scientific method" is one example. Amore complex qualification comes fromhis introduction, stating, "It should be emphasized that this essay is of necessity tentative and preliminary; I do not pretend to answer all the questions that I raise" (p. 218).

• Wordplay: Sokal engages in wordplay that gives a nod to the French deconstructionist pedigree of *Social Text*. Some examples of this type of critical wordplay that reveal contradictions and reversals within seemingly unitary meanings include Sokal's repeated use of the term "(w)holism" to describe quantum gravity, as well as the following sentence: "Suffice it to say that anyone who has seriously studied the equations of quantum mechanics will assent to Heisenberg's measured (pardon the pun) summary of his celebrated uncertainty principle" (pp. 218-219).

• Jargon: Sokal whips out all of the cultural-studies jargon, including but not limited to the following major buzzwords: hegemony, domination, emancipatory, dialecticism, deconstruct, transcend, ideology, capitalistic, problematize, and transgressing. Significantly, he also used scientific jargon, such as "Planck-scale" and "open strings," that was probably unfamiliar to cultural-studies scholars—just as 19th-century scientific hoaxers like Poe and Locke laid an impenetrable veneer of astronomical jargon over their hoaxes to lend them an air of scientific authority.

Citation. Sokal clearly did his homework on who was involved in and fashionable with the Social Text editorial collective.

- Among a ludicrously weighty 20 pages of notes and references (which *Social Text* editors unsuccessfully requested that he cut down)(Robbins & Ross, 2000, p. 55), Sokal cites Marxist and socialist critics Althusser, Aronowitz, and Jameson; French postmodernists Deleuze and Guattari, Derrida, Irigaray, Serres, Lacan, and Lyotard; science-studies critics Haraway, Harding, and Latour; and in addition to Aronowitz, *Social Text* editor, Andrew Ross.

- Sokal went beyond simply structuring a skeleton of typical cultural studies references; he fleshed it out in the text of the hoax by making bold, sweeping claims, capped off with parenthetical citations—a convention of *Social Text* articles—thus forcing his readers either to view the notes or look up the cited studies if they wished to see the actual data supporting the claims. For example, in his discussion of differential topology and homology, Sokal structures his support as follows:

"Furthermore, as Lacan suspected, there is an intimate connection between the external structure of the physical world and its psychological representation qua knot theory: this hypothesis has recently been confirmed by Witten's derivation of knot-invariants (in particular the Jones polynomial [Jones 1985]) from three-dimensional Chern-Simons quantum field theory (Witten, 1989). (p. 225)"

- Sokal does not explicate knot theory or any other technical terminology, nor does he show how they support his argument in an endnote. Eliding the data and the interpretation from this support structure is convenient shorthand but blocks non expert readers' abilities to evaluate his claims until they have had the opportunity to look up Jones' and Witten's studies.

The excellent fit of Sokal's rhetorical strategies to the Social Text paradigm suggests that he made explicit efforts to satisfy editorial expectations. That the hoax was accepted for publication is, of course, not necessarily proof that these strategies were the sufficient causes of its acceptance. As we will explain shortly, the editors could have had reasons for publishing the article that were relatively unrelated to its rhetorical virtuosity, for instance, their subscription to the ideologies it performed. However, the hoax's rhetorical mimicry of the typical Social Text article certainly encouraged the editors' receptions of it as a standard contribution to their journal. In particular, Sokal exploited the cultural-studies convention of short handing citations—providing the reader with only a bald claim of support and a citation while eliding the data and the interpretation that connects them—to work in dozens of nonsensical claims that the editors never took the time to verify. He hoisted them on their own-conventions.

EXAGGERATING AND VIOLATING EXPECTATIONS

If the editors had been able to read past their own preconceptions, could they have been able to detect the hoax? We think they might have, had they paid close attention to the stylistic and the generic features of the text that Sokal submitted. Rhetorical sensitivity to persistent generic and stylistic exaggerations within the text of Sokal's article might have averted the embarrassment suffered by the editors, had they been able to adjust their vision. The generic features Sokal mimicked were often not merely mimicked but were parodically exaggerated. A method of analysis that might help us parse some of that exaggeration is Gricean (1975) analysis of implicatures. Implicatures can also be seen as conventions, similar to the specific, generic conventions detailed above, but they apply very generally to all cooperative communication. They state that, in general, a communication adheres to the maxims of quantity (say only as much as is needed); quality (say only what is true); relevance (what you say should be pertinent to the matter at hand); and manner (do not speak ambiguously or unclearly). Of course, people flout these so-called rules all the time for effect, and in the context of speech, we learn how to interpret the messages that such floutings convey. Ordinarily, whenever a maxim is flouted, it is done publicly to create a very specific effect that the hearer knows how to recognize. So if we ask someone how her day was, and she rolls her eyes and says with sarcastic intonation, "Great!" we know to interpret her statement ironically; she is clearly flouting the maxim of quality. On the other hand, if she smiles and says "Great!" with an enthusiastic tone of voice, and yet her day was terrible, she is violating quality (i.e., she is lying to us). Violating, unlike flouting, involves a maxim being broken privately and therefore uncooperatively by the rhetor.

Sokal certainly violated quality in his hoax, because he submitted many logically false statements with the appearance of truth (and because he submitted his entire article, which was a fake, as a genuine article). However, he also included several flouting of maxims in his article, which the editors might have been able to catch if they had been reading carefully. For instance, although Sokal's article was of a conventional length for a journal submission, its heavy citation and notation was clearly distended, a flouting of the maxim of quantity. Although we know the editors took note of this exaggeration because they asked for cuts, their final decision to publish the article unchanged indicates that they may have interpreted the excessive documentation not as parodic exaggeration but rather as evidence of the super conscientiousness of a disciplinary outsider eager to show that he has done his homework. Their desire to sign up a particle physicist to their cause, as Sokal surmised, may have driven the selection of this self-flattering interpretation over one more consistent with the maxim of quantity.

In addition to quantitative analysis, we can also identify some floutings of the maxim of manner. Certainly, Sokal mimicked the complexity, abstraction, difficulty, and jargon of cultural-studies rhetoric, but we can still ask whether the exaggeration might have been caught by vigilant editors. Most journal editors, in the experience of most academic writers, keep an eye out for excessive jargon. The very title of Sokal's article ("Transgressing the Boundaries:

" Toward a Transformative Hermeneutics of Quantum Gravity") is exaggeratedly conventional or, we might say, hyper-normal. The sheer jargon-per-square- inch ratio should have alerted editors that Sokal was parodying their field. A further quantitative exaggeration of a generic feature is the presence of not one but two epigraphs to the article, the doubling not itself a guarantee of parody but certainly an inflation of the academic article's genre's characteristics. The first epigraph violates the maxim of manner in that it is ambiguous, referring either to Sokal's daring venture outside the sanctuary of his own field as he dons the regalia of science studies (the editor's evident interpretation) or to his own subversion of science studies: "Transgressing disciplinary boundaries . . . [is] a subversive undertaking since it is likely to violate the sanctuaries of accepted ways of perceiving" (1996a, p. 217)".

 Indeed. In another quantitative exaggeration, the editors might have noted with suspicion—but evidently did not—the article's great number of complimentary references to their own work (13 to Aronowitz's alone). Although the parodic dimension of such extravagance is striking from a perspective outside of science studies, from the editors' perspective (one that flattered themselves, of course), they must have looked like the outsider's or the beginner's attempt to earnestly reproduce the conventions of a discipline he could not claim as his own.

Aside from such quantitative violations, does Sokal's article contain floutings of quality (i.e., ironic statements)? What should the editors have made of the following? "Mathematically, Einstein breaks with the tradition dating back to Euclid (which is inflicted on high school students even today!), and employs instead the non-Euclidean geometry developed by Riemann" (1996a, p. 221). Even if one did not recognize the banality of the statement that geometry is still taught in high school, the exclamation point itself—the written equivalent of an eye roll or of a casting up of the hands—might have been a giveaway. Or what about a sentence like the following: "Thus, a liberatory science cannot be complete without a profound revision of the canon of mathematics. As yet no such emancipatory mathematics exists, and we can only speculate upon its eventual content" (p. 231)? Should the oxymoron "emancipatory mathematics" have triggered editorial suspicion, or would the editors have been so taken by the paradox (a figure common in academic writing) that they would not question the sense of the juxtaposition? Much of Sokal's article weaves and juxtaposes quotations from critics and from philosophers whom he considers especially abstruse, and it can be argued that one person's abstruseness might be another's careful scholarship. Still, it is hard to miss the irony of the introduction to the following sentence quoted from Deleuze and Guattari:

"In quantum physics, Heisenberg's demon does not express the impossibility of measuring both the speed and the position of a particle on the grounds of a subjective interference of the measure with the measured, but it measures exactly an objective state of affairs that

Sokal introduces this leviathan: "As Gilles Deleuze and Felix Guattari so lucidly point out, . . ." The detection of irony, of course, depends on the assumption that rhetor and audience share certain basic values and attitudes, and in this case, the irony evidently went undetected because Sokal maneuvered the editors into assuming that they did when they actually did not. Even if the editors found the sentence incomprehensible and were evidently bullied into agreement by Sokal's assumption that Deleuze and Guattari's statement is lucid if he pronounced it lucid, they would risk seeming unsophisticated by challenging that judgment. The question then becomes, Who is the more sophisticated reader: Sokal or the editors? The irony folded back and bit the editors.

Textual cues such as those unpacked in the preceding analysis, as well as reader-unfriendly conventions like shorthanded citations, all became crucial anchors for Sokal's later arguments about culturalstudies scholars' fuzzy thinking and careless appropriation of scientific language. In the end, however, as a hoaxer, he could not have wished for the editors of *Social Text* to pick up on his clues. If they had, his article would never have been published, the hoax would have failed, and he would never have gained the national platform from which to attack those whom he perceived as his adversaries. Sokal counted on his adherence to the conventions of cultural studies to blind the editors to his trick, just as the tailors counted on the emperor's pride to blind him to his own nakedness. In a reply to Michael Bérubé about the affair, Sokal (2000) excuses himself for injecting a military metaphor into his summery of the editorial over- sight: "Acting not as intellectuals seeking the truth, but as self appointed generals in the "Science Wars," they apparently leapt at the chance to get a 'real' working scientists on their 'side' (p. 144). Sokal (1996b) had made this accusation once before in his original revelation in *Lingua Franca*:

"The editors of *Social Text* liked my article because they liked its conclusion: that "the content and methodology of postmodern science provide powerful intellectual support for the progressive political project." They apparently felt no need to analyze the quality of the evidence, the cogency of the arguments, or even the relevance of the arguments to the purported conclusion. (p. 64)".

It is interesting to note that Robbins and Ross's response to Sokal after the affair came to light corroborates the physicist's accusation about their political agenda. In answer to the question, What could they have been thinking?, they replied that "from the first, we considered Sokal's unsolicited article to be a little hokey"

(2000, p. 54). The word choice is noticeable—hokey meaning naïve? overenthusiastic in an unsophisticated way? corny?7 They thought Sokal was "awkwardly but assertively trying to capture the 'feel' of the professional language of this field, while relying upon an armada of footnotes to ease his sense of vulnerability." Basically, they figured Sokal a rookie trying to enlist in their movement. That they viewed his enlistment as a notch in their belts is clear, as they labeled his contribution "unusual" in coming from a natural scientist and therefore "worth encouraging" (p. 55). In otherwords, it was worth it for them to risk publishing a dodgy article if it came with a stamp of scientific support for their endeavor. Faced with stylistic howlers, the editors chose to read them innocently, in the way that flattered their own position. Their overvaluation of position—both their own and Sokal's—produced inattention to textual evidence of an infelicitous communication situation.

It is hardly news that, as Jonathan Culler (1980) says, "reading is not an innocent activity" (p. 116) and that even such a seemingly private act as editorial reading (without referees) can be infected at the core by political and social agendas. American writers of scientific media hoaxes noted this phenomenon as early as 160 years ago. In 1835, Edgar Allan Poe complained bitterly about the outshining of his first moon hoax, "Hans Phaall," by Locke's (1835) "Moon Hoax." He claimed that the science of Locke's hoax was vastly inferior to his own but that newsreaders' love of novelty and of sensation overwhelmed their logical faculties as they read the hoax and led them to believe it (Poe, 1846, p. 161). Mark Twain riddled his 1863 "Empire City Massacre" hoax with factual inconsistencies that should have been glaringly obvious to local newsreaders, yet it fooled many of them and led to an outcry for his dismissal from the *Territorial Enterprise* once it was revealed. In one of the earliest recorded reading protocol experiments, Twain (1870) reports sitting in a café and watching one farmer reading his hoax aloud to another:

"I saw that the heedless son of a hay-mow was skipping with all his might, in order to get to the bloody details as quickly as possible; and so he was missing the guideboards I had set up to warn him that the whole thing was a fraud. (p. 861)".

"Twain concludes,

I found out then, and never have forgotten since, that we never read the dull explanatory surroundings of marvelously exciting things when we have no occasion to suppose that some irresponsible scribbler is trying to defraud us;we skip all that, and hasten to revel in the bloodcurdling particulars and be happy. (Twain, 1870, p. 861)".

Twain was arguing that readers' predispositions largely determine the reading experience. Specifically, he was arguing that the farmers' high valuations of sensation blinded them to the story's logical inconsistencies.

Sokal seems to have counted on a similar dynamic when he tailored his article for the *Social Text* editors. He counted on their expectations that scientists tell the truth to trump any suspicions that might arise about the inconsistencies and the inaccuracies in his article. He counted on his readers to be flattered by his reproduction of the jargon and the politics characteristic of cultural studies. Sokal, like Poe and Twain, figured the hoax-reading experience as a competition among readers' assumptions about the genre, the so-called real world, and the political world. The interpretation of the hoax that readers arrive at tells us those assumptions that are predominant. The revelation of the hoax lays open the readers' most dearly held assumptions and values to public scrutiny.

Thus, Sokal (1996c) exploited the editors' unthinking subscriptions to certain leftist ideologies and to rhetorical conventions, such as obscure shorthanded citations and scientized jargon, as a platform from which to launch a generalized and a massively public criticism of the new Left for being intellectually lazy and thereby abandoning the serious work, criticism, and oversight of science to capitalist interest groups in America (p. 344).

In the end of this example we can conclude that Sokal did the hoax prove? Or, more precisely, what did it prove about science studies, and does it have any significance beyond that subdiscipline? In the narrowest sense, we can say with some certainty that if it proved anything, it proved that the editors of *SocialText* were not as conscientious and as savvy as they thought they were. Even though *Social Text*, as they claimed, was not a scholarly refereed journal but what they call a journal of opinion produced by an editorial collective, they should have vetted the article by sending it to a physicist. In addition, they ought to have picked up on the article's so called hokeyness, which they were all too willing to attribute to the eagerness of a scientist to be accepted into their club. But finally, *Social Text* is not a large target. The journal continues to publish and continues to speak to its audience. It can plausibly be argued that, in the long run, *Social Text* was only embarrassed and that no careers were destroyed, though academics do not take embarrassment kindly.

As a rhetorical event, the Sokal hoax offers some implications for rhetorical criticism. Our approach to the hoax and to the controversy that ensued from it, although not taking up some of the larger philosophical questions it raised, points out the importance of sensitivity to text, to context, and to genre for all parties—hoaxers, readers, critics, and respondents.Without awareness of the double audience that the hoax produced, we would be unable to distinguish the hoax's first phase, with its sharp recriminations fromthe allies of *Social Text*, from its second phase, during which the hoax was widely read as a parody and thus became widely available as fodder for a barrage of attacks on leftist academia.Without a conception of the hoax as a genre of social interaction, we would also be confounded by Sokal's seeming ambivalence about the scope of his attack and the message he wanted to deliver. And finally, without knowledge of the way a hoax functions rhetorically—its parasitism on the conventions of the genre it is aping—we would have been unable to appreciate both Sokal's successful mimicry of the conventions of cultural studies and his flouting of more general rhetorical conventions governing communication. The rhetorical context of the Sokal hoax produced its long life and its intense political fallout; counterbalancing rhetorical attention to text might have prevented the incident. But then again, those in a position to pay careful attention to text were preoccupied by consciousness of their own position within their field, a disciplinary nearsightedness that led them to misread the position of the perpetrator. Sokal's hoax, and all media hoaxes, teach us that the very act of reading is an inescapably social and rhetorical event; it is a political statement, an affirmation of group membership, and a continual reconstruction of moral, ethical, and public reality. Although the guideposts for its unmasking were all present in Sokal's hoax and were all evident to Sokal and to later readers, in the end, the editors of *Social Text* could not remove their assumptions, as if they were simply a pair of sunglasses, and the editors read the words on the page without filtering them through their own filters of self-importance. They—we—can certainly try to keep our preconceptions from blinding us, and it is a noble effort. But savvy hoaxers like Sokal know we will fail. A clever magician can hide an elephant right in the middle of the stage by getting people to look in one direction while he blindsides them from another.

Rumoring in newspapers

The problem of appearance and perception of rumors is of great interest of many psycholinguists, sociolinguists and researchers of other scientific fields who study different aspects of influence on (Dmitriyev, Latynov & Khlopyev 1997; Le Bon, 1998; Pendleton, 1998; Olshansky, 2001; Zheltukhina, 2003; Knapp, 2004; Miller, 2006; Slyshkin & Chizh, 2008; Zheltukhina & Omelchenko, 2008; 2011, etc.). The analysis of factual material (printed and media)

The concept "rumor" is perceived as coming from one or more people information statement about some events than are not officially confirmed, it is conveyed orally from one person to another and orally or in written through communication media (Zheltukhina & Razmerova, 2010). Rumors deal with important for particular social group events, correspond its needs and interests.

Perception and reproduction of heard information are caused by dissatisfaction of needs and their expectation for being satisfied.

Spreading rumor is a result of collective creation, collective attempt to explain problematical and emotive situation. The concept "media rumors" are the information message proceeding from one or more persons about some not confirmed officially events arising spontaneously or created artificially distributed.

Literature Review

The problem of mass communication in Russia, especially in sphere of mass information is traditionally studied in theory of speech, sociolinguistics, psycholinguistics, the theory of influence, stylistics. Beginning with middle 70s of the 20th century texts functioning in the sphere of mass communication are recognized as a matter of interdisciplinary research dealing with the problems of defining the status of language of mass media, ways of describing media-texts of different types, determination of the role of language, texts of mass media in the process of formation of language and speech culture of its native speakers (Zheltukhina, 2010; 2011; Slyshkin et al., 2014). The studying of media texts in cognitive-discursive paradigm and linguacultural aspect is related to new approaches. Today the most popular approaches are comprehensive approach, considering language of mass media as a matter of interdisciplinary research (Zasursky, 2008) and systems approach allowing us to see the matter of research in its specified integrity (Zheltukhina, 2010). Integral theoretical comprehension of media communication has become possible only nowadays. Multifold approach to the matter of interest allowing us to change extensive methods and describing techniques to intensive studying of media discourse and more systematic its conception was developed thanks to references to processes of language functioning under different conditions, language comprehension as anthropological phenomena. The change from mono-logical communicative paradigm of totalitarian society (one person says, other listen to him and accomplish) to dialogical paradigm of pluralist society affected media discourse, caused journalists' communicative freedom consisting of abundance of innovations, preference for unusual forms of thoughts` expression, widening of standard language limits and sometimes even deliberate violations of language standards. Such communicative freedom allowed printed mass media to present a large amount of unchecked or distorted information and rumors using lexical, grammatical and stylistic means (Zheltukhina, 2011; Dobronichenko et al., 2012; Borodina & Zheltukhina, 2015a, 2015b, Zheltukhina et al., 2016b; Zheltukhina et al., 2016c).

through Review of publications on the subject showed that works of domestic and foreign linguists in the field of comparative linguistics, sotsio-and psycholinguistics, pragmalinguistics, cognitive linguistics, cultural linguistics, stylistics, rhetoric, of the theory of journalism, and also the theory of discourse, the theory of influence, the theory of rumors have formed theoretical base of the researches.

methods of the analysis. In news, we should apply the following methods: inductive, descriptive and comparative, cognitive and discursive, semantic, definitional, functional and stylistic analysis.

A methodological basis of work is system approach. According to the principles of system approach, any phenomenon is considered as integrity in unity of all its communications and relations. For the complex analysis of rumors in a modern media discourse, verbal means of rumors impact on the addressee in modern foreign-language and Russian mass media linguacultural, linguapragmatic,

discursive approaches are used.

Examples of hoaxing and rumoring in news:

California Governor Jerry Brown In the Middle of a Corruption Investigation

https://www.google.co.uk/search?num=50&safe=off&ei=S2FFWsCGO8iZgAbipb2ACg&q=California+Jerry+Brown+Corruption+Investigation++-fake+-snopes&oq=California+Jerry+Brown+Corruption+Investigation++-fake+-snopes&gs_l=psy-ab.3...17611.28381.0.28595.57.55.2.0.0.0.117.3066.49j4.53.0....0...1c.1.64.psy-ab..5.0.0....0.b3xOKXYJ9H8

Clinton / Lynch Pilot Breaks His Silence on What Was Said

https://www.google.co.uk/search?num=50&safe=off&biw=1545&bih=792&ei=NG5GWqntAeWQgAa1q7fgBQ&q=Clinton+%2F+Lynch+Pilot++-fake+-snopes&oq=Clinton+%2F+Lynch+Pilot++-fake+-snopes&gs_l=psy-ab.3...978.2040.0.2168.8.8.0.0.0.0.53.383.8.8.0....0...1c.1.64.psy-ab..0.0.0....0.rD-vkEezMOE

Illegal immigrants started California Wildfires

https://www.google.co.uk/search?num=50&safe=off&rlz=1C5CHFA_enGB744GB744&biw=1381&bih=866&ei=OAxFWvusBOqP0gLsu7uoDw&q=Illegal+%22immigrants%22+start+California+Wildfires+-fake+-snopes&oq=Illegal+%22immigrants%22+start+California+Wildfires+-fake+-snopes&gs_l=psy-ab.3...11208.15641.0.16080.12.12.0.0.0.0.116.732.10j1.11.0....0...1c.1.64.psy-ab..1.0.0....0.XryMdrN8xCk

Black Lives Matter 'Thugs' Blocked Emergency Crews from Reaching Hurricane Victims

https://www.google.co.uk/search?num=50&safe=off&ei=1wVFWuOYFKKH_Qbm96PgBQ&q=Black+Lives+Matter+%27Thugs%27+Hurricane+Victims&oq=Black+Lives+Matter+%27Thugs%27+Hurricane+Victims&gs_l=psy-ab.3...27926.34703.0.35679.3.3.0.0.0.0.81.213.3.3.0....0...1c.1j2.64.psy-ab..0.1.81...0i10k1.0.0agDvP_r9kg

Democrat Principle Defecates In Front Of Students During Pledge of Allegiance

https://www.google.co.uk/search?num=50&safe=off&rlz=1C5CHFA_enGB744GB744&biw=1545&bih=792&ei=aXFGWuiXCMKNgAbBlqv4Cg&q=principal+defecates+in+front+of+students+-snopes+-fake&oq=principal+defecates+in+front+of+students+-snopes+-fake&gs_l=psy-ab.3...820.3046.0.3160.20.17.3.0.0.0.135.1353.12j5.17.0....0...1c.1.64.psy-ab..0.2.183...0j33i21k1.0.qOlAGaV33wU

Palestinians Recognize Texas as Part of Mexico

https://www.google.co.uk/search?num=50&safe=off&rlz=1C5CHFA_enGB744GB744&biw=1545&bih=792&ei=2GxGWoqsJ6KcgAbBnL-QAg&q=Palestinians+texas+%22part+of+mexico%22+-snopes+-fake&oq=Palestinians+texas+%22part+of+mexico%22+-snopes+-fake&gs_l=psy-ab.3...1791.4215.0.4388.2.2.0.0.0.0.52.96.2.2.0....0...1c.1.64.psy-ab..0.0.0....0.Ijec5GDTO90

Hillary Clinton's Assistant J.W.McGill Found Dead

https://www.google.co.uk/search?num=50&safe=off&ei=D2NFWqXdN4nPgAaFurmlBw&q=Clinton+McGill+dead++-fake+-snopes&oq=Clinton+McGill+dead++-fake+-snopes&gs_l=psy-ab.3...13021.19697.0.20051.22.22.0.0.0.0.74.1053.22.22.0....0...1c.1.64.psy-ab..0.0.0....0.7oPosSIX8vc

FBI Issues Warrant for Obama's Arrest After Confirming Illegal Trump Tower Wiretap

https://www.google.co.uk/search?num=50&safe=off&ei=LGVGWsKBPYvagAaet6H4Dw&q=FBI+warrant+for+Obama+arrest+wiretap+-snopes+-fake&oq=FBI+warrant+for+Obama+arrest+wiretap+-snopes+-fake&gs_l=psy-

ab.3...17868.26032.0.26224.43.39.3.0.0.0.105.2003.38j1.39.0....0...1c.1.64.psy-ab..2.0.0....0.al4-r3eUuHc

Paul Ryan: "Women Who Use Birth Control Are Committing Murder"

https://www.google.co.uk/search?num=50&safe=off&ei=IWVGWrilA-CogAagnLDYBA&q=%22paul+ryan%22+%22birth+control%22+murder+-snopes+-fake&oq=%22paul+ryan%22+%22birth+control%22+murder+-snopes+-fake&gs_l=psy-ab.3...8979.10850.0.11154.2.2.0.0.0.0.51.97.2.2.0....0...1c.1.64.psy-ab..0.0.0....0.MspY-Qio-GU

Pragmatic analysis of news

Through a review to the above news, we explore the Building further on the founding's until now, we will focus on the linguistic features of fake news headlines, and if they hold any predictive power regarding the distinction between fake and real news. The prime reason for investigating news headlines is because that is the factor that prompts a consumer to read an article. Due to a lack of a reliable dataset with a large magnitude to be able to experiment properly, news statements will be explored that are used in news as well. It will be seen to what extent the classifier trained on the statements apply to headlines because of the absence of a clean dataset when it comes to labeled news headlines. Thus, the research question is: What are the linguistic features of fake news statements and headlines that make it distinguishable from real news and make it propagate? In order to give a proper answer to the question, it is essential to address the following sub-questions that will help shape up the outcome.

- Which methods can be used to extract linguistic features?

- How does wording affect the distinction between fake and real news?

- Which linguistic features have the most predictive power regarding propagation and distinction?

The expectations are that linguistic features do in fact hold predictive power and are able to decently distinguish between fake and real news headlines. In the researches, and language models appear to be used to extract linguistic features. Along with that, it seems that certain words help the distinction, especially when it comes to propagation. Mostly, Hence, sub-questions shall aid in finding the answer to the questions. This research shall first discuss related work that will assist in enhancing the methodology, which will be elaborated after that. By extracting linguistic features and using classifiers on them to be able to predict if a statement or headline are fake or not. On the basis of the extensive approach, the results will be presented.

1. With the use of pragmatic analyze, explored the effects of changing the wording of a news regarding its degree of propagation. The data used consisted of news from several sources that posted but with different wordings. These features were mostly linguistic ones, such as informative (length) and requests to share, a words ("please", "pls share"). pragmatic analyze was applied to the news. Eventually, the relevant features were: length, verbs, proper nouns, numbers, positive words, indefinite articles, and adjectives. These discovered features that influence propagation can be used to explore if they also apply to fake news statements and headlines.

2. Contrarily, the goal was to classify fake news and determine if left- and right-wing are more alike than mainstream news. The BuzzFeed Fake News dataset, which contains articles manually fact-checked by journalists, was used. To inspect if left- and right-winged publishers are more alike, Unmasking was used. Features that were used were: n-grams, stop words, POS tags and dictionary features. Ultimately, classifying fake news was a complicated task. This conclusion arose from the fact that the accuracy was less than chance. However, making a distinction between hyperpartisan news and mainstream news yielded promising results. This paper gives an indication that classifying fake news still has a long way to go and there is certainly a need for better features that apply to fake news. It will definitely assist with constructing a base of linguistic features and attempting to attain a better result than this.

3. Satire and hoax news are closely related concepts, so similarly in Rubin et al. the goal was to distinguish satire from real news by using textual features of satire. The dataset consisted of satirical news articles and matching legitimate news articles. Machine learning was used for the prediction and the experiments were conducted by using several combinations of features to determine the best performing combination. measures were used as a baseline. The highest measure was achieved when grammar, punctuation, and absurdity were used. Individual textual features of syntax and punctuation marks are a reliable indication of the presence of satire. Along with that, satire news mostly consists of complex sentences .The result was that

headlines are very relevant to detect satire, since the first line of satirical articles repeat the content of the headline, whereas real news packs new information. Additionally, sentence length and complexity were pretty vital as well. The success of the above features might also prove to be beneficial for fake news and statements. A large problem in combating fake news is the lack of datasets. In order to improve that complication, Wang (2017) created the LIAR dataset, consisting of 12791 political statements by politicians, labeled with how true or false they are. The labeling process has been done by Politifact.com editors, a website dedicated to debunking political rumors. These statements can be used for fake news detection, as stated by the author. Also, because of the large size of the dataset, it can be used for machine learning problems. By using logistic regression, SVM and bi-LSTM, the aim was to find out if surface-level linguistic features do have some kind of influence. The six-way classification consisted of the following classes: pants on fire, false, mostly false, half true, mostly true and true. Using word-embeddings they achieved an accuracy of around 25% with SVM and logistic regression, while bi-LSTM appeared to suffer from over-fitting. Another task was to see if a hybrid approach with meta-data would yield better results.

From the points above , several features and algorithms can be used to analyze the linguistic properties of the headlines of fake news and what makes it propagate. To find linguistic differences between fake and real statements and headlines, features will be extracted on semantic and syntactic levels. Below, there is a list of features, with an explanation of what they stand for. The manner of extraction for features . Many of these are inspired from features that have been discussed in section (related work) and have turned out to be helpful for related areas.

- Amount Sentences: How many sentences does the item contain?
- Length: How long is/are the sentence/sentences on a word-level?
- Mood: Is the statement/headline indicative, imperative, conditional or subjunctive? Amount Capital Letters: How many capital letters does the sentence contain?
- Ratio Capital Letters: How many capital letters does the sentence contain, in comparison to the amount of words? This, because abbreviations tend to consist of capital letters only. Hence, the ratio is taken to get a feel of how much balance there is in the sentence.
- Amount Punctuation Marks: How many punctuation characters are there?
- Punctuation Marks: Does the sentence contain any punctuation marks? Done per punctuation symbol.
- Amount Quotes: What is the amount of quotes in the statement or headline?
- Average Quote Length: The summed up length of the quotes, divided by the amount of quotes.
- Sentiment: Is it a positive or negative statement?

- Subjectivity: How subjective is the statement? This ranges between the values of 0 and 1.

- Likelihood of words: How rare is the occurrence of the words used in the sentence. Also till $n = 2$.

- Commonness of words: How many common words are used in the sentence?

- Amount of definite articles: How many times does the word the occur in the sentence? This gives an indication of the generality. Amount of indefinite articles: How many times do the words a and/or an occur in the sentence? This, as well, gives an indication of the generality.

Another feature explored in these news is the commonness of words . To be able to find the commonness, a likelihood model is developed over the Reuters Corpus retrieved from nltk. This method has been used in Danescu-Niculescu-Mizil et al. (2012) as well, where they used the Brown Corpus instead. By using language models, insight is gained in the complexity of words and Part-Of-Speech tag sequences. Thus, does a sentence contain more prevalent words and/or syntax or unusual wordings and/or sentence structures? The language model built over the Reuters Corpus is then used to calculate the likelihood for each sentence. A lower likelihood indicates a lesser occurrence, while a higher likelihood makes it more likely for the sentence to occur.

Additionally, a different method for the same type of feature was used, where the frequencies of words occurring in the Reuters Corpus was investigated. A cut-off frequency value k was taken, where when looping over a sentence in the dataset, the frequency of each word in that sentence is looked up in the Reuters Corpus. Comparing the frequency with that of k, if it is equal or larger (which means that the word is rather common), the total common score of the sentence is increased with 1. If it is lower than k, the total common score of the sentence remains the same.

Conclusion

1. Now that it is clear which features will be used, the method of extraction shall be explained. Not all the features will be explained because of the triviality of some, e.g. length of a headline or presence of punctuation marks.

2. The findings of this research reinforce the fact that fake news detection is a difficult task to tackle and needs more research. Such as Potthast et al. (2017) and Wang (2017).

3. Something to be noted is the difficulty of being able to tell what is fake and what is real. Biases might play a role in the determination, as well as a lack of knowledge of events that have played out and/or how. As can be seen in the self-annotated headlines dataset, there is no such label as half-true. This is because of the limited expertise regarding the field, which made it hard to establish if something is just half-true or not.

4. In the future, a proper dataset of a large magnitude might enable more space for research with diverse data. Along with that, it might be useful to combine NLP-techniques with information retrieval and reinforcement learning to see if those hybrid-approaches improve the distinction. Other linguistic features such

as the amount of spelling and grammar mistakes can be experimented with as well.